Simple Machines

by Martin E. Lee

PEARSON
Scott
Foresman

DK

What is a machine?

Work

In science, work does not mean doing homework or chores. Work means using force to change or move something. The force can be a push or a pull.

How can you use a lot of force but not do any work? Suppose you push very hard on a brick wall. No matter how hard you push, you won't move the wall. Nothing moved and nothing changed. So you didn't do any work. Something must move or change for work to be done.

Machines make work easier

A machine can be just one piece, or it can have many parts. Some simple machines help so you use less force to do a hard job such as moving heavy things. It takes more force to move a heavy object than a light one.

Other simple machines change the direction of force. You may push or pull in one direction. The simple machine helps you by changing the force to a different direction.

Some simple machines have just one or two parts. But they can help you do work. The lever, the wheel and axle, and the pulley are simple machines. The inclined plane, the wedge, and the screw are also simple machines.

Levers

A **lever** is a long bar on a support. The support is called the **fulcrum.** The object you want to move is the **load.** A push or a pull on the bar that makes the load move is the **effort.**

A lever adds to your force. It can also change the direction of the force.

The effort and the load on Lever A below are both four units from the fulcrum. The effort used is equal to the downward force of the load. The load on Lever B is closer to the fulcrum. You use the same effort to balance a larger load.

You can use math to show how a lever helps effort. Multiply effort by the distance from the fulcrum. The product is equal to the load times its distance from the fulcrum.

Effort	×	Distance	=	Load	×	Distance
4	×	4	=	8	×	2
	16		=		16	

Lever A

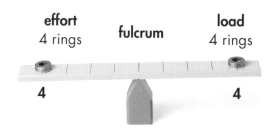

effort
4 rings   fulcrum   load
4 rings

4   4

The fulcrum of Lever A is the same distance from the load as from the effort.

Lever B

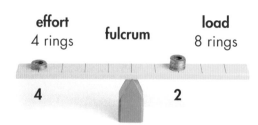

effort
4 rings   fulcrum   load
8 rings

4   2

The fulcrum of Lever B is closer to the load than it is to the effort. The same effort balances a larger load.

Types of Levers

You can sort levers into three groups. The fulcrum, load, and effort are in different places in each group.

Groups of Levers

Some levers have two bars that work together.

Group 1

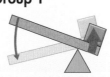 

The fulcrum of the pliers is between the effort and the load. The effort is where you squeeze. The load is the object the pliers are squeezing.

Group 2

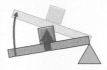 

The fulcrum of the nutcracker is at the closed end. The effort is at the open end, where you squeeze. The load is the nut to be cracked.

Group 3

The fulcrum of the tongs is at the closed end. The load is at the open end, where you grab objects. The effort is between the fulcrum and the load, where you squeeze.

Wheel and Axle

The **wheel and axle** is a special kind of lever. It moves or turns objects. The axle is a rod. It goes through the center of the wheel.

A screwdriver is a good example of a wheel and axle. The handle is the wheel. The metal blade is the axle. The end of the blade fits into the top of a screw. You use force to turn the handle. The blade turns and tightens the screw.

Screwdriver

A doorknob is another kind of wheel and axle. You use force to turn the knob. The knob is the wheel. This force is increased as it turns the small axle. The axle is the turning shaft inside the doorknob. Turning a doorknob allows you to open and close a door.

Look at the picture of the hose reel. The crank is the wheel. It is joined to the axle, which goes through the center of the reel. You use effort to turn the crank. With each turn, you wind up more of the hose. Soon you wind all of the long hose onto the reel. And it was easy to do!

Doorknob

Garden hose reel

Pulley

A **pulley** is a wheel with a rope, wire, or chain around it. The pulley in the picture below is actually two pulleys. The top one is fixed in place. The bottom one moves up and down with the load.

A pulley changes the direction of force. In the picture, the force scale is measuring the force needed to raise the weight. The weight is pulling down on the pulley. The pulley changes the direction of the force. When you pull the hook at the end of the force scale down, the weight goes up.

You can reduce the amount of force you need to move a load by using two or more pulleys together. Look at the picture. There is only one length of rope between the top pulley and the force scale. But there are two lengths of rope between the pulleys. Both ropes carry weight. This means that less force is needed to lift the load.

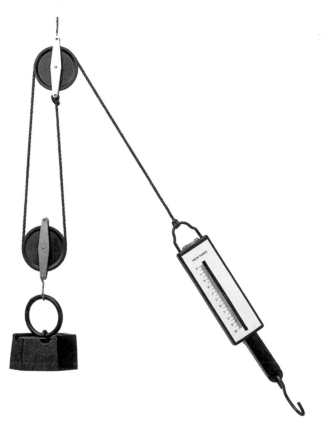

Block and Tackle

Two or more pulleys make a system of pulleys. If one of these pulleys is fixed in place, the compound pulley is called a block and tackle. Adding more pulleys to the system reduces the effort you need to lift a load. Using more pulleys allows you to use the same force to lift more weight. The system on the left uses one pulley to lift a smaller weight. The system on the right uses more pulleys to lift a larger weight.

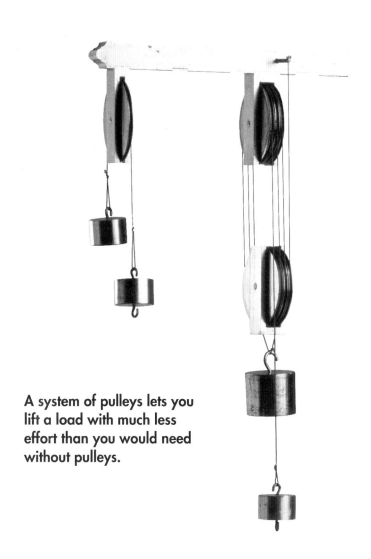

A system of pulleys lets you lift a load with much less effort than you would need without pulleys.

How can machines work together?

Inclined Plane

Suppose you are trying to get a very heavy box of books onto your desk. The box is too heavy to lift. You might try pushing it up a ramp instead of lifting it. You could use a long, sturdy board for your ramp. Pushing the heavy object up the ramp would be easier than lifting it.

A ramp is a simple machine called an **inclined plane.** You use the same total force to lift an object straight up as you do when you slide it up an inclined plane. But with an inclined plane, you don't have to apply the force all at once. You apply less force over a longer distance.

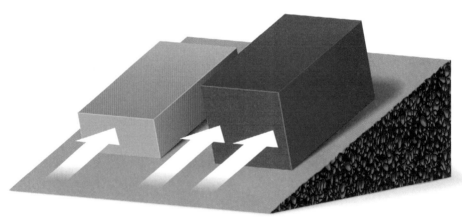

Pushing the smaller box up the inclined plane takes less force than pushing the larger box up the same inclined plane.

Factors that Affect Force

Objects can move up or down on an inclined plane. It takes more force to move an object up a short, steep ramp.

Friction is a force that exists between two surfaces that rub against each other. Friction can slow things down. It makes it harder to drag, push, or slide objects.

A box at the top of a ramp stays there. Why? The force of friction balances the downward force of gravity. But suppose you put wheels on the box. Wheels take away most of the friction. The force of friction is now weaker than the pull of gravity. The box rolls down the ramp.

You need more force to move a heavy box up a ramp than you need to move a light box. Using more force allows you to move an object faster.

Less force is needed to go up inclined planes that aren't very steep.

More force is needed to go up a steep inclined plane.

11

Wedges

A **wedge** is a special kind of inclined plane. It is two inclined planes in the shape of a V. Usually a wedge must move to do its work. A force is applied to the wider end of the wedge. This makes the wedge move forward. The force drives the thin edge of the wedge into an object.

Wedges are used to move or split things apart. Sometimes wedges are used to hold things in place.

Look at the picture below. The force of the hammer pounds against the wider end of the wedge. This force drives the pointed end of the wedge into the wood. The wedge changes the downward force of the hammer into a sideways force. The sideways force splits the log apart.

This wedge stops large objects from moving.

Screws

A **screw** is a small rod with slanting ridges wrapped around it. These ridges are called threads. The screw is a type of inclined plane. If you could unwrap a screw's threads, you would clearly see the inclined plane, pictured below.

Screws have many uses. They can lift things. They can hold things in place. A screw holds pieces of wood together better than a nail does. Why? A nail can slip out. But the threads make it hard to pull out a screw.

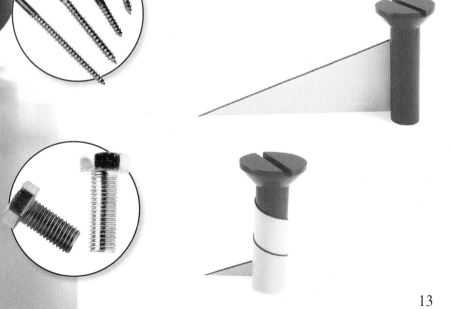

Complex Machines

You can put simple machines together to do bigger or harder jobs. Complex machines are made of two or more simple machines that work together.

You may have a can opener in your kitchen. Is it like the one shown here? Look at it closely. Do you see the simple machines that make it work?

The circles you see may be wheels and axles. Some of the wheels have spikes or points. They are gears. The spikes are called teeth. Gears are often used in pairs. They change the speed or direction of motion.

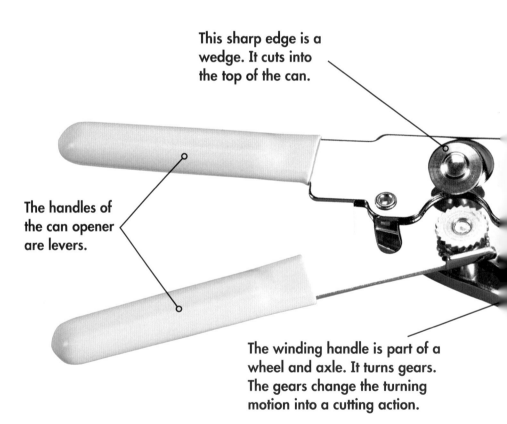

This sharp edge is a wedge. It cuts into the top of the can.

The handles of the can opener are levers.

The winding handle is part of a wheel and axle. It turns gears. The gears change the turning motion into a cutting action.

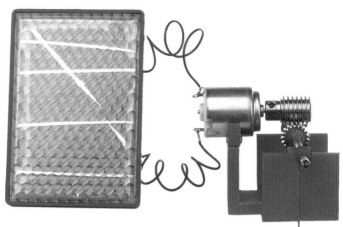

Here is another complex machine. It has a different power source than the can opener does. The can opener needs your muscle power. This machine gets its power from the Sun. The box on the left holds solar cells. These solar cells change energy from the Sun into electric energy that powers the machine.

Look at the rest of the machine. You can see wheels and axles. You can see gears. How do you think the gears change the direction of motion?

The machine is lifting a heavy load. The lifting part is a simple machine. Which one is it?

There are many kinds of machines. Some are simple, and some are very complicated. But they all help us do work with less force. They make our lives easier in many ways.

Glossary

effort a push or pull that makes a load move in some way

fulcrum the support on which a lever and its load rest

inclined plane a simple machine also called a ramp

lever a simple machine made of a bar on a fulcrum

load an object to move

pulley a simple machine made of a wheel with a rope, wire, or chain around it

screw a simple machine made of an inclined plane wrapped around a rod

wedge a simple machine made of two inclined planes put together in the shape of a V

wheel and axle a simple machine that turns in order to move objects